Editor
Kathleen Kehl Lewis, M.A.

Editorial Project Manager
Ina Massler Levin, M.A.

Editor-in-Chief
Sharon Coan, M.S. Ed.

Illustrator
Wendi Wright-Davis

Cover Artist
Sue Fullam

Art Coordinator
Cheri Macoubrie Wilson

Creative Director
Elayne Roberts

Imaging
Ralph Olmedo, Jr.

Product Manager
Phil Garcia

Publisher
Mary D. Smith, M.S. Ed.

MsMitura

How to Give a Presentation

Grades 6–8

Author

Michelle Breyer, M.A.

Teacher Created Resources, Inc.
6421 Industry Way
Westminster, CA 92683
www.teachercreated.com

ISBN: 978-1-57690-501-2

©1999 Teacher Created Resources, Inc.
Reprinted, 2007
Made in U.S.A.

Table of Contents

Introduction

How to Give a Presentation offers a series of speaking and listening activities to introduce students to a variety of ways to present material to a group. This book takes students through the steps necessary to prepare and organize presentations.

Use this book as a springboard for enriching oral language learning in all subject areas. You may want to combine some of the methods presented to create new activities and add additional material of your own. Be creative and have fun with these materials. Soon your students will say with enthusiasm and confidence, "I can give a presentation!"

This book is divided into the following sections:

Organizing and Preparing Presentations

Students are given the tools to organize, prepare, and practice presentations.

Let's Be Informed

Students are provided with many methods to present biographical, geographical, and historical information.

I Can Show You How

Students demonstrate their "know-how" by using a wide range of techniques.

Persuasive Arguments

Students learn the fine art of rhetoric through group and individual persuasive presentations.

Improvisation

Students participate in activities that will help them "think on their feet."

Tell Me a Story

Students have the opportunity to explore their dramatic, storytelling skills.

Tech Talk

Students are introduced to forms of multimedia that allow them to enhance presentations they give.

Thoughts on Prewriting

Unless you are giving an impromptu speech, you need to know how to plan ahead for your presentation. Prewriting is a good way to organize your thoughts and actions for your final presentation. However, before you begin one of the following types of prewriting activities, it is important to know exactly what kind of presentation you are planning to give. The following is a list of questions that should be answered before choosing a prewriting activity, as well as suggestions for using this book for various presentations:

1. **What is the goal of your presentation?**
   - Are you trying to show your knowledge of a certain topic, person, place, or event? If so, *brainstorm* (page 5) for research ideas and use the *Informative Presentation Organizer* (page 7). For suggestions on different ways to present your information, refer to the sections "Let's Be Informed" and "Tech Talk."
   - Are you going to demonstrate how to make or do something? If so, *brainstorm* (page 5) for the materials you will need, as well as the sequence of steps needed to demonstrate and use the *Demonstration Presentation Organizer* (page 8). For suggestions on different ways to present your demonstration, refer to the section "I Can Show You How."
   - Are you trying to persuade your audience to like something, change their point of view, or believe that something is better than something else? If so, *brainstorm* (page 5) for arguments that support your position and use the *Persuasive Presentation Organizer* (page 9). For suggestions of different ways to present your view point, refer to the section "Persuasive Arguments."
   - Are you telling a story? Are you acting out a scene from a story or an event in history? If so, *brainstorm* (page 5) for ideas and use the *Autobiographical Incident Presentation Organizer* (page 10) or the *Story Presentation Organizer* (page 11). Use the pages on *Storyboards* (page 12) or *Scripts* (pages 13 and 14) to help with special effects and stage directions. For suggestions on different ways to present your story, event, or scene, refer to the section "Tell Me a Story."

2. **Will you be giving this presentation alone, with a partner, or in a group?** Make sure you select a presentation technique appropriate for your situation. If you are working with a partner or in a group, part of your prewriting plan includes who is responsible for each task. Read the information on *Scripts* (pages 13 and 14) to help plan your group presentation.

3. **Do you want to include props, visual aids, audio, or other special effects?** Use the page on *Storyboards* (page 12) to help organize effects and insert them into your presentation.

4. **What do you do once you have planned your presentation and written it out?** No first draft is perfect! What looks good on paper doesn't always work as a presentation. Complete the "Postwriting Activities" and "Practice Makes Perfect" before presenting in class.

5. **How will you be graded on your presentation?** Talk with your teacher to find out the exact requirements for your presentation. You may be graded on the content of your presentation as well as your presentation skills. A *Presentation Evaluation Form* (page 19) has been included in this book as a suggestion for evaluating and improving oral presentation skills. The form can be used by the teacher and/or peers.

Brainstorm

One of the first tools as you plan your presentation is to *brainstorm*. To begin, think of your topic and the goal of your presentation (see page 4). Write down every idea that comes to you, no matter what. Don't judge any of your ideas or think that any idea is too unimportant. Sometimes it's the little ideas that lead to really great ideas! When you think you have run out of ideas, take a deep breath and keep writing. Sometimes the flow of ideas slows and then picks up again. When you are sure you have no more ideas or you have enough that you like, then you can look more carefully and just pick the ones that you think will make the best presentation. Here are two different ways to *brainstorm* your ideas on paper:

1. **Lists:** Some people like to randomly list ideas as they flow from their heads. Then they can go back and organize the list into sections or categories appropriate for a presentation. Below is a list generated for an autobiographical presentation about the worst vacation ever:

Colorado	16-hour drive	trailer locked	fixing trailer in rain
stormy	dark, stormy clouds	crying sister scary	walk to dinner
bad camp spot	river gully	no gas	lost gas cap
boat fixed	ski rope broke	thunder	rain
no sleep	cold water	fighting kids	cold chicken

2. **Webs and Clusters:** Webs and clusters are another way to *brainstorm*, but instead of just listing ideas, you place them on your paper in relation to each other with lines connecting ideas. Begin with your topic in the center of the cluster and branch off with ideas or specific details. Below is a cluster or web generated for an informative presentation on the different species of early humans:

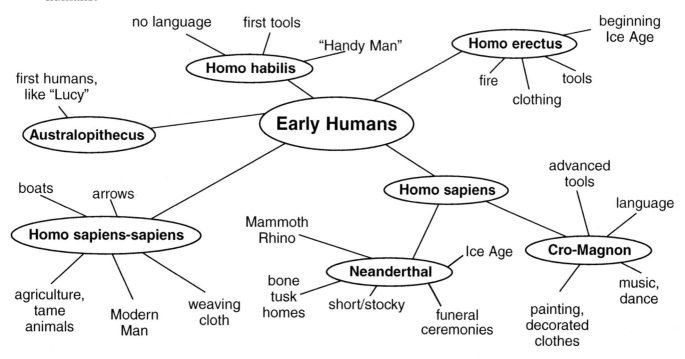

Outlines and Organizers

Another way to plan for your presentation is to make an outline or use an organizer. This type of prewriting can be done while or after you *brainstorm* (page 5) to help sequence your ideas into an organized format. Below is an example of an outline for an informative presentation. Pages 7–11 offer organizers for the different types of presentations described in this book. Choose the appropriate organizer for your presentation, or develop an organizer of your own that fits your presentation guidelines.

Outlines

Many writers prefer to begin with an outline. To make an outline, choose two or more main ideas and assign them Roman numerals: I., II., III., etc. Next, divide each main idea into subtopics and give each of these its own line and letter: A., B., C., etc. These subtopics may require their own divisions; if so, they are assigned Arabic numbers: 1., 2., 3., etc. If these need further division, they will be labeled with lowercase letters: a., b., c., etc.

<table>
<tr><td>

Outline

I. Introduction
II. Body
   A. First Subtopic
      1. Description of the subtopic
      2. Further information on the subtopic
         a. a detail about the information in 2
         b. another detail
   B. Second Subtopic
      1. Description of the second subtopic
      2. Further information on the second subtopic
   C. Third Subtopic
      1. Description of the third subtopic
         a. a detail about the description
         b. another detail
      2. Further information on the third subtopic
III. Conclusion
   A. Summary of Subtopics
   B. Concluding Remark

</td><td>

Example Outline: '60s Fads

I. Introduction
II. '60s Fads
   A. The Beatles
      1. Their origins
         a. The Cavern
         b. Liverpool
      2. Their first tour of America
      3. Their music
   B. Fashions
      1. The miniskirt
      2. Go-go boots
      3. Granny dresses
   C. Hippies
      1. Clothing and hairstyles
      2. Lifestyles
III. Conclusion
   A. '60s Summary
   B. Concluding Remark

</td></tr>
</table>

Informative Presentation Organizer

Introduction and Attention Getter

The opening statements let the audience know who you are and what you are going to talk about. To begin, you can share a joke, ask a question, or describe some interesting trivia relevant to your topic that will get the attention of your audience. Reveal to your audience the reasons your topic is of interest to them, why it is relevant, or what they can learn. Then list the three main points you are going to discuss during your presentation. Use the back of this paper to organize this part of your presentation.

Body of Presentation

This is the majority of your presentation. Describe each main point with at least two to three supporting details.

Main Point 1	Supporting Details
Main Point 2	Supporting Details
Main Point 3	Supporting Details

Conclusion

Summarize your three main points, refer to your introduction, and end with a strong closing statement.

_____

_____

_____

Demonstration Presentation Organizer

Introduction and Attention Getter

The opening statements let the audience know who you are and what you are going to talk about. To begin, you can share a joke, ask questions, show a visual aid, or describe some interesting trivia related to your topic that will get the attention of your audience. Then introduce yourself and explain what you are going to demonstrate during your presentation. Use the back of this paper to organize this part of you presentation.

Body of Presentation

This is the majority of your presentation. It should include the materials needed, the sequence of steps, and the purpose or why someone might want to do what it is you are demonstrating. You do not need to present each category in this given order, yet all three categories should be covered completely by the end of your presentation.

Materials:_____

_____

_____

Steps: _____

_____

_____

_____

_____

Purpose: _____

_____

_____

Conclusion

Summarize your demonstration and end with a strong closing statement referring to the information in your introduction.

_____

_____

_____

Persuasive Presentation Organizer

Introduction and Attention Getter

The opening statements let the audience know who you are and what you are going to talk about. To begin, you can tell a joke, ask a question, or describe some interesting trivia related to your topic that will get the attention of your audience. Then introduce yourself and describe the issue at hand. Tell your position on the issue and list the three main reasons for your position. Use the back of this paper to organize this part of your presentation.

Body of Presentation

This is the majority of your presentation. Describe each reason with at least two or three supporting details. Make sure each reason is truly different and separate.

Reason 1	Supporting Details
Reason 2	Supporting Details
Reason 3	Supporting Details

Conclusion

Summarize your three reasons and end with a strong and convincing closing statement.

_____

_____

_____

_____

Autobiographical Incident Presentation Organizer

Think about the event from your life that you are planning to retell to the class. Make sure it is an event that clearly illustrates your understanding of the assignment. Use the organizer below to help present your thoughts clearly.

Introduction and Attention Getter

The opening statements let the audience know who you are and what you are going to talk about. You can share a joke relevant to the event, ask a question (Have you ever?), or begin with an interesting and exciting part of your story that will get the attention of your audience and introduce your event. Organize this part of your presentation below.

_____

_____

_____

_____

Body and Sequence of Main Events

This is the majority of your presentation. It must include a clear sequence of what happened, the setting of the event, and the reactions and feelings of the characters involved. Make sure you highlight the climax of your event with details and gestures.

1. _____

2. _____

3. _____

4. _____

5. _____

Conclusion

Summarize by describing at least three reasons why this event was especially memorable to you. Then give a strong closing statement.

_____

_____

_____

Story Presentation Organizer

Introduction

Character Description: _____

_____

Setting Description: _____

_____

Problem of Story: _____

_____

Plot

Sequence of Events: Describe obstacles/conflicts/scenes leading to the climax.

1. _____

2. _____

3. _____

4. _____

Climax

Describe the exciting scene in which the problem is solved.

_____

_____

_____

_____

Conclusion

What happens after the problem is solved?

_____

_____

_____

_____

Storyboards

Storyboards help you to plan a presentation that will use visual aids (objects, pictures, videos, slides, etc.), actions (gestures, stage directions, etc.), and/or audio (recorded music, sounds, speaking, etc.). You can use this storyboard form or create your own storyboard based on your presentation guidelines.

Outline of Presentation	Visual Aids	Actions	Audio
Introduction			
Main Body			
Conclusion			

Scripts

A script is most commonly used when acting out a play or story. However, a script can also be helpful for any type of presentation with two or more presenters. There are three main elements to writing a script:

- Characters—The names of the characters should appear at the top of the script, as well as in front of the lines each character is speaking.
- Dialogue—The dialogue, or words the characters are saying, is written without quotation marks.
- Stage directions—Directions for expression, gestures, movement, props, or scenery are written inside parentheses.

Following are two examples of scripts. Note how the characters, dialogue, and stage directions are organized. The first script is the beginning of a play about the afterlife in Ancient Egypt:

Characters:	**Narrator**	**Horus**	**King Ptuh**	**Thoth**
	Ammit	**Osiris**	**Anubis**	**Maat**

Narrator: Long ago in Ancient Egypt, the priests mummified the dead so that they were preserved for their afterlife in the Field of Reeds, the Egyptian form of heaven. Yet before they could enter this magical place, the spirit of the deceased had to pass a test of honor called "The Weighing of the Heart." Join the spirit of King Ptuh as he enters the underworld with the assistance of the god Horus and his trusty *Book of the Dead*.

(Curtain opens to reveal a chamber with paintings and hieroglyphics on the walls. In the center of the room is a large, but fake, scale. Anubis, the jackal-headed god, stands at one end of the scale. Thoth, the ibis-headed god, stands at the other end holding a tablet and stylus. Sitting on one end of the scale is a small girl with a feather on top of her head. She is Maat, the goddess of truth. Over in the corner sits the little monster Ammit. He growls occasionally. Horus enters the chamber leading the spirit of King Ptuh. Under the king's arm is the Book of the Dead.)

Horus: Come my friend! You have used wisely your spells from the book to help you through the passageways. Not one monster was able to defeat your charms! And now we stand before the scales, the last test before meeting the great Osiris, Lord of the Dead. (*Pats the king on the back and presents him to Anubis.*)

Anubis: Welcome King Ptuh! (*Ammit lets out a fierce growl. The king shakes with fear.*) Never mind the little beast in the corner. If you have lived a good life of honor and truth he shall once again go hungry. (*Stepping towards king and looking him over suspiciously.*) But I see you tremble. Perhaps you have cause to fear Ammit. Is it possible you are not worthy to enter the Field of Reeds?

Thoth: Let us get on with it, dear Anubis! This soul is trembling with the fear of the unknown, and I have recorded his reaction. What humble soul ever enters our chamber without trepidation? It is only the foolish and dishonest who mock us with their confidence. (*Point to the empty scale end.*) Enter the scale, King Ptuh!

(The king sits on the scale end fearfully. Yet, because it is a fake scale, his end does not rise higher than the end holding tiny Maat. The king reacts joyfully.)

Scripts (cont.)

The next example script shows the beginning of an informative group presentation about the afterlife in Ancient Egypt. Note how the organization and format are the same, even though the group is not putting on a play.

Characters: **Colton**   **Kara**   **Rich**   **Michelle**

Colton: (*Standing in front of the table.*) Have you ever wondered where we get the saying, "I'm feeling *lighthearted*" or "He must have done something really bad to have such a *heavy heart*"? Both of these sayings come from the Ancient Egyptians and their mysterious ceremony of the dead called (*mysteriously*) "The Weighing of the Heart."

(Play Egyptian music as Kara, Rich, and Michelle enter, Egyptian style, with a poster showing "The Weighing of the Heart" ceremony. Turn music down. Colton, Rich, and Michelle place the poster on the board as Kara finishes the introduction from behind the table. All visual aids and props needed for the presentation have been placed on the table in front of the room.)

Kara: Welcome. My name is Kara. (*Point to each as they are introduced.*) Colton, Rich, Michelle, and I are here to tell you about the fascinating beliefs of the Ancient Egyptians in regards to the afterlife. Today you will learn about the *Book of the Dead* and traveling to the Underworld (*hold up the book)*; "The Weighing of the Heart" ceremony (*point to the poster);* and meeting Osiris, the Lord of the Dead, who granted permission to enter into the Field of Reeds, the Egyptian form of heaven. (*Hold up the picture of Osiris.*)

Rich: After a person died, it was believed that his or her spirit traveled through a series of guarded passageways underground. In order to choose the right path and defeat the monstrous guards, the spirit used spells and incantations from the *Book of the Dead (hold up book).* That is why the book was usually included in the tomb of the deceased during the burial process. Here is an example of advice from the *Book of the Dead. (Read passage on page 231.)*

Michelle: Usually, the spirit was also guided by the hawk-headed god Horus, son of Osiris. *(Show a picture of Horus.)* Once the spirit and Horus made their way through the secret passageways, they came to the weighing chamber. . . .

Proofreading, Editing, and Revising

Proofreading

When you first write or plan a presentation, you should feel free to be creative. Don't worry if spelling is correct or even if your ideas are good enough. Just keep planning and writing, using the prewriting pages to help with the organization. Once you have a first draft of what you plan to say and do, you can check to see if you made any sense. Go over your work two or three times and check for understanding and clarity, as well as mechanical errors such as spelling, grammar, and sentence structure. Be sure to read out loud what you have written so you can truly hear if you made errors.

Editing and Revising

At this point you are ready to have someone else check your work. Although the presentation might make perfect sense to you, you need someone who is objective to catch errors in transitions, discover omissions of information, and keep all of the information clear. Use the *Presentation Edit Sheet* (page 16) and have two different people help edit your presentation. The first editor should just listen to your presentation and focus on the content. Was the information clear? Did you include all of the requirements? Did you use clear sentences with rich details and descriptions? Have the first editor make comments on the edit sheet and help you make the corrections on your first draft itself.

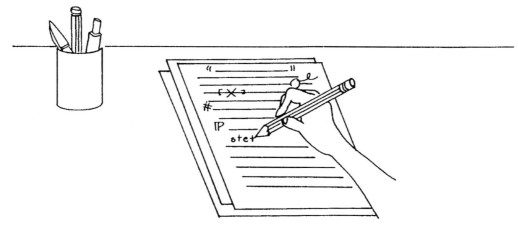

The second editor will read your work to help with mechanical errors such as spelling, grammar, and sentence structure. Remember, you can make corrections on your first draft. Circle words or phrases that you want to check. Cross out anything that does not work. Draw arrows to show where to move a phrase that would work better someplace else. Many people find it helpful to skip lines when writing a first draft so that they have plenty of room for editing and revising. Like the first editor, the second editor should write comments on your edit sheet and help make corrections directly on your first draft.

Once you have met with both editors, it is time for your final revisions. It may be that all you have to do is rewrite using the notes, additions, and scribbles that appear on the first draft. As you work, you may have more ideas for making your presentation even better. That's okay. Editing and revising are ongoing processes that keep recycling until you are pleased with the final product. However, creating is a process that never ends. With each project you do, you learn more about how to make the next one even better.

Presentation Edit Sheet

Name_____   Title of Presentation _____

+ = Excellent   ✔ = Okay   ✳ = Problem (Editors will help make corrections.)

	1st editor Listen and revise.	2nd editor Read and revise.
Proper presentation format? Introduction, body, conclusion?		
Details and descriptions? Adjectives, figurative language?		
Correct sentence structure? Run-ons, choppy?		
Correct grammar and word use?		
Good transitions from point to point?		
Strengths of the piece?		
Weaknesses? (Editors help make needed corrections.)		
Names of editors		

Practice Tips

Once you have a final draft of your presentation, it is time to practice. If you are planning to use visual aids, actions, props, audio, etc., it is important to make a note of these directly on your final draft. See the planning pages for *Storyboards* and *Scripts* (pages 12–14) to help insert special effects.

At first you can practice by reading through your presentation word for word, making the appropriate gestures or facial expressions. Do this several times until you feel comfortable with your content and presentation. Once you feel like you have the content well memorized, it's time to move on to cue cards.

Cue Cards

If you are presenting alone, large index cards work well as cue cards. On the cards you should write a brief outline of your presentation and any cues for action, props, visuals, etc. Remember, you cannot READ your presentation, so it is better if you do not have your word-for-word copy in front of you. If you are working in a group, it might be possible for someone to sit offstage and hold up large cards or construction paper with brief notes explaining what comes next. This is how it is done in the movies and on TV.

Practice and Feedback

Practice will help you feel more confident and comfortable speaking in front of an audience. You may find it helpful to practice in front of a mirror or even to videotape a rehearsal and review it. If possible, have a test audience, such as a small group of friends or your family, listen to you. Use the feedback from your practice runs to edit and revise as needed.

It is also important to know how you are going to be evaluated so that you can practice all of the necessary items. Are you being graded only on the content of your presentation, or will you be graded on using visual aids, gestures, and eye contact? Check with your teacher to make sure you understand the guidelines of the assignment. A *Presentation Evaluation Form* (page 19) has been included as a sample for evaluating the organization, content, and technique of a presentation.

Tips for Success

1. Practice enough so that you only need a few notes. Try to speak freely and naturally without getting away from your organization.

2. If you do need to refer to your cue cards, be sure to lift your head up as much as possible so that the audience can see and hear you clearly.

3. Avoid using slang and unclear speech. Practice pronouncing each word clearly, without slurring.

4. Practice the speed of your speaking and vary it throughout the presentation to add interest. Don't speak rapidly, like you would to a friend on the telephone. When you have several people listening, it takes a bit longer for your message to get across. However, don't speak so slowly that your audience falls into a hypnotic trance. Make sure you insert a pause to emphasize a point before moving on to the next point.

Practice Tips *(cont.)*

5. Practice the volume of your speaking. Sometimes when you get nervous you speak softly. Although it may feel like you are shouting at times, make sure you are loud enough to be heard in all areas of the audience. Perhaps your teacher will signal you if you are not loud enough.

6. Try not to look stiff and awkward like a robot. Try to act naturally and use animated gestures and facial expressions. It's okay to move around and use your hands while speaking, but be careful not to move around too much or your audience will focus on your movements and forget to listen.

7. Instead of thinking of a speech as a form of cruel and unusual punishment, write a speech that you will enjoy giving. Try to think about what you would like to see and hear if you were sitting in the audience. You may find a way to include the audience by asking questions, or you may entertain them by telling a joke related to your topic.

What to Do About Stage Fright

1. First of all, remember that most people get some "butterflies" or nervous feelings when they stand in front of an audience. So remember that your nervousness is normal.

2. If you are really nervous, you can imagine that you are a famous actor or actress just playing a role. Or imagine that everyone in the audience is really nervous and you are not nervous at all.

3. You might try choosing two or three friendly faces in the audience to focus on from time to time. Just don't forget the rest of your audience.

4. Remember, the best medicine for stage fright is practice. The more you practice, the more you will feel comfortable and confident!

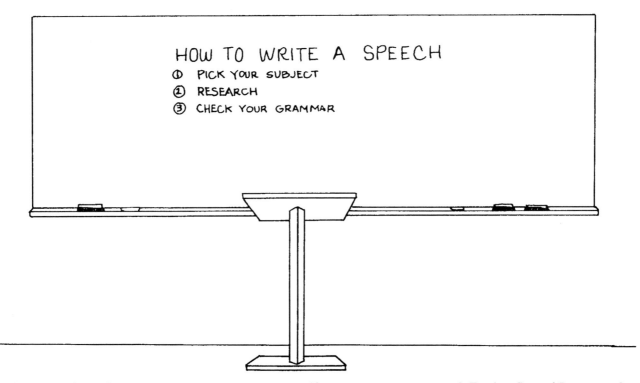

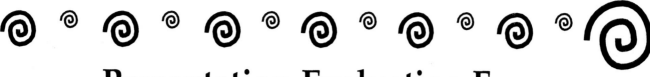

Presentation Evaluation Form

Speaker _____ Evaluator _____

+ = Excellent   ✔ = Okay   ✳ = Problem area (Needs improvement.)

Place an evaluation mark in each category, along with constructive comments.

Organization and Content:

Introduction (background to gain interest)	
Body (details and descriptions)	
Conclusion (summary and closing statement)	

Technique:

Voice expression (volume and inflection)	
Clear and complete sentences without run-ons	
Correct grammar (no slang or "um," "like," "you know," etc.)	
Eye contact (looks at audience and not notes)	
Gestures	
Visual aids	
Prepared and rehearsed	

Time (3-minute minimum): _____

What did or didn't keep your attention?_____

_____

Best part of the presentation: _____

_____

Suggestions for improvement on the next presentation: _____

_____

_____

Introduction to Informative Presentations

One of the fundamental principles of any presentation is to inform the audience. Yet, one can also be entertaining and interesting while getting information across. To successfully present a basic informative speech alone or in a group, it is important to plan ahead. The information must be broken into subtopics or points and sandwiched between an interesting introduction and conclusion. See the opening section on "Organizing and Preparing Presentations" as it pertains to informative presentations.

This section also contains some creative ways to present your information by using dramatic flair. In the first activity, *Living Statues* (page 21), students relate their biographical information while dressed up as famous characters or statues in a museum. This is an excellent way to present historical biographies for social studies or characters from literature. For example, the class could take a visit to the Fairy Tale Museum, the Museum of Early Man, or The Greco-Roman Museum of Art.

Another way to present information as a character is to *Bring a Book Report Alive* (page 21). In this activity a student dresses up as the main character from a story and gives the book report from that character's point of view. The book can be a biography about that character or a novel with a notable main character. As an extension, students could work in small groups to re-enact scenes from a story, as in *Drama on the Spot* (page 36) or *Writing Dialogue* (page 38).

Interviews (page 22) are also an interesting way to present biographical information. Students can work in pairs or in small groups to create an interview broadcast formatted like a variety show, tabloid show, news show, or press conference. Examples of questions and topics for discussion have been provided.

Informative presentations also teach the audience about a time period, event, place, hobby, pastime, animal, science topic, etc. A straightforward informative speech with visual aids and props would convey this information well. However, if you are looking for a change of pace, try one of the following formats. In *Let's Talk About It* (page 23), students work in small groups to create a talk show about a certain topic. One student acts as a famous host who invites experts on the topic to join the show for the day. Another "show" format is described in *Game Show Host* (page 23). One student is the leader of the game show, and information is presented while players pretend to play the game.

If it is a place you are reporting about, such as a state, a country, a new settlement, a region in the ancient world, etc., then a presentation in the form of a *Travelogue* (page 24) may be an appropriate alternative. In this activity, students can present their information as if they are taking a journey to the place, or they can create an informative and appealing commercial to make others want to visit the place. As an extension, a small group of students may wish to create a *News Broadcast* (page 38) to further discuss the different features and activities of the place.

The final activity is an entertaining way to present the evolution of a time period for a story. In *Living Time Line* (page 24), a group of students puts on a fashion show to describe the changes that took place during the time period of the story. For example, the fashion show could depict the evolution of government in Ancient Greece, the changes in colonial attitudes, or the emotions of characters throughout the story. For ideas on easy costumes or scenery for any of the activities above, see "Send In the Props" (page 41).

Informative Presentations

Living Statues

This activity is an entertaining alternative to a standard biographical speech. Although you will plan and prepare your own biographical information (See the *Informative Presentation Organizer*, page 7.), the presentation of the information will be done in a group with each student taking a turn speaking. Select a famous person to research, and then prepare a brief informative speech about the person's life. Your teacher may wish to assign characters from the historical period you are studying, characters from the literature you are reading, or allow you to read a biography of your choice.

Once you have prepared your speech, your teacher will assign you a day and time for you to present your information. You will be taking a journey to a special museum where the statues come alive! On the day of your presentation, you should dress as your character. Your teacher will arrange the speakers around the classroom and have them freeze as if they were statues. With the lights turned off, a flashlight will let the statues know when it is their turn to come alive and give their speech.

(Teacher's note: The teacher can "ham it up" by pretending to be the museum guide leading the class to the different statues! Allow several days so that each student has a turn in the museum. A group of five or six students per day works well.)

Hercules

Orpheus

Perseus

Bring a Book Report Alive

Book reports can be dull and boring to write, let alone read. You will give an oral book report in which you take on the persona of the main character. Plan your presentation based on the criteria of the teacher's book report. Use the "Organizing and Preparing Presentations" section, beginning on page 4, to help get organized and prepare for visual aids or props.

On the day of your assigned presentation, dress as your main character. As you present your information, you should attempt to talk, move, and act like the character you are portraying. The delivery of the report should also be from that character's point of view.

You could also be assigned a biographical book report. In this you would dress as your character and give an informative presentation based on the character's life. See the *Informative Presentation Organizer* (page 7) to plan a biographical presentation.

Interviews

Informative Presentations

Conducting an interview with a partner or a small group is an interesting way to convey biographical information. You can pretend to conduct a press conference, talk show, tabloid show, or news broadcast. If desired, you can videotape the interview or add slides, music, visual aids, and props. See the opening section on "Organizing and Preparing Presentations" for information on using a storyboard (page 12) and writing a script (pages 13 and 14).

Below is a list of suggested topics and questions for interviews:

Introduction

Open the broadcast for your show in the proper manner for your format and introduce the character being interviewed. Possible introduction topics might include the following:

- name
- time period
- where the character lives
- family
- occupation or position

Body of Interview

Decide ahead of time at least three main points you want the audience to learn about this person. Possible topics might include the following:

- what most makes the person famous
- achievements
- personality traits
- people who helped along the way
- feelings about life
- relationships
- style of leadership
- conquests
- why the person made certain decisions
- what it feels like to be famous
- what the person wished he/she had accomplished but didn't
- how he/she died
- if the person could live in a different time or place, where it would be and why

Conclusion

Wrap it up by summarizing the main points covered in the interview, and allow the character to give the final closing words that he/she feels epitomizes his/her life. Close the broadcast in the proper manner for the format you have chosen.

Informative Presentations

Let's Talk About It

One way to convey information about a certain topic is to plan a presentation in the form of a talk show. Work in small groups to design a talk show with a famous host and guest experts. The show should have an introduction, main body, and conclusion just like an informative speech, yet different people will be discussing the different parts. For example, in place of a speech on volcanoes, the talk-show host could introduce a geologist to discuss the features of a volcano and how they are formed, a person who lived through a volcano eruption could discuss the effects, and a volcanic scientist could discuss detection techniques for future eruptions.

You can also videotape your show or add special effects. See the opening section on "Organizing and Preparing Presentations" for information on planning, organizing, adding effects using a storyboard (page 12), and writing a script (pages 13 and 14). Dress-up in costumes for your show and use gestures and expressions appropriate for your characters.

Game Show Host

Another entertaining way to present information is in the format of a game show such as Jeopardy. (There are many popular game shows for children today on TV. Discuss the formats of these shows to see which ones best lend themselves to presenting the information clearly.) Using this format, the game show host will introduce the players and the topic for the day. The categories for questions will be the main points the presentation is to cover. The players will play the game, revealing correct and incorrect information. Points will be awarded as on a real game show. At the end of the presentation, when all of the topics have been covered, a winner will be selected. The winner can then summarize the topics of the informative presentation, and the game show host can give a closing statement.

Review the opening section on "Organizing and Preparing Presentations" for ideas on planning, organizing, adding effects, and writing scripts. Remember, although it is in the format of a game show, it is really just an unusual and entertaining informative speech!

Demonstration Presentations

Demonstration Duos

Have you ever watched a cooking show or home improvement show? Most likely the demonstrations were done by two people working together. Work with a partner to create an episode of some kind of demonstration show. You could do a spin-off of a favorite show already on TV or create your own original format. Ideas for shows include teaching how to cook, make crafts, create art projects, make home improvements, or play a sport.

Use the information in the first section on "Organizing and Preparing Presentations" (page 4) to plan your episode. You will need the *Demonstration Presentation Organizer* (page 8), as well as the pages on *Storyboards* (page 12) and *Scripts* (pages 13 and 14). Your show should open with some music, the title of your show, and an introduction of the two stars. After you have completed your demonstration and given the concluding remarks, close your show with a farewell and catchy saying. Then play the exit music while you show the "credits," or who did what. If desired, you could videotape your episode and play the final product in class just like a real TV show!

Time Capsule

Have you ever wondered what life must have been like for kids 100 to 1000 years ago? Don't you wish you could pop in a video and be transported back in time? Imagine how helpful it would be for future historians and archaeologists to come across a video that demonstrates exactly what life was like for students in your day and age! Together with your class, brainstorm a list of things to demonstrate what would illustrate life at school, play, and home. The list might include some of the following:

Daily home routines: making the bed, brushing your teeth, setting the table, preparing breakfast, doing the dishes, cleaning the house, taking care of a pet, doing homework.

Home recreation: playing a board game, playing computer games, listening to music, talking on the phone, watching TV or movies.

Daily school routines: coming and going to school, entering and exiting the classroom, teaching a lesson on the different subjects you are studying, classroom discipline, special classroom activities.

Outdoor activities: sports, games, "hanging-out," riding bikes and skateboards.

Think about how life has changed for kids over the last 100 years. What would a student from 1890 think about your laptop computer or video games? What would they think about the subjects you learn in school and your life at home? Now imagine how out of date the technology, school subjects, customs, pastimes, and fashions from today will be in 100 years! Things as simple as a toothbrush or as sophisticated as a Sony PlayStation™ will change dramatically in 100 years, so don't leave anything out!

For your Time Capsule, design a video format with an introduction, main body, and conclusion. Use the opening section on "Organizing and Preparing Presentations" to help with your planning. If possible, your teacher will allow individual students or partners to tape their segments separately. Then, edit the entire video together onto one tape. Place the tape into a box with other significant items from your year, along with names, phone numbers, and addresses of all the people involved in the video project. Plan to open the box again in 20 years and review your work!

Demonstration Presentations

Post It!

Have you ever tried to put something together by following a diagram and set of directions? If you have had both good and bad experiences, you understand the art of giving good directions! Try your hand as a direction writer by creating a demonstration poster. Think of a simple craft, building project, drawing subject, or other skill that could be easily taught by using a few diagrams and written directions.

Use the *Demonstration Presentation Organizer* (page 8) to plan your demonstration poster, and then draw your diagrams and write your directions on a few sheets of paper. Have a friend or two attempt to follow your directions without any help. Use their feedback to edit and revise your diagrams and directions. Once you feel your directions are clear, draw and write them on a large sheet of poster board. Make sure there is a title at the top and your name on the bottom. Make the poster attractive and colorful, yet neat and clear.

Present your poster by giving a demonstration speech. Use the same organizer you used to plan your poster (page 8), but this time add a catchy introduction and conclusion. Follow each of the steps and show your progress.

(Teacher's note: After the class speeches are completed, hang up the posters and try some of the activities described!)

Make a Paper Airplane

1. Fold paper in half to make a crease.

2. Fold each corner into the middle.

3. Fold each top edge in towards the middle-line even with the center crease.

4. Now fold paper in half.

5. Fold the side(s) down about half way-these are the wings.

6. Level the wings out straight . . . ready for take off.

by Colton James

Demonstration Presentations

Slide Show

Sometimes a demonstration is impossible to show in person because it is time consuming or involves a need for a large space. One way to give a demonstration presentation without actually demonstrating is to narrate a slide show. You can plan your slide show as an individual, partner, or group project.

Brainstorm (page 5) to decide on a good topic for demonstration, and then organize your demonstration (*Demonstration Presentation Organizer*, page 8). When you know what it is you want to do, you need to plan a storyboard. You can use the chart on page 12, or you can design one of your own with plenty of room for each slide you plan to show.

To begin the storyboard, write an outline for the introduction, the directions for each step of the demonstration, and the conclusion. Make sure you move to a new space each time you plan to show a new slide. Then draw a simple picture in each space to represent the photo you plan to take in correspondence to the outline. If you plan to add music or other effects, note them on the storyboard, as well.

Have someone help you edit and revise your storyboard before you spend money on film. Once you feel ready, go out and photograph! Make sure you are using transparency film in your camera that will make slides. Refer to your storyboard to take the photos. Since not all pictures will come out as planned, take a few photos of each shot. When the film has been processed, choose the best ones and put them in order.

Next, you can add your narration and any sounds or music. If you plan to speak while your slides are shown, see the section on *Scripts* (pages 13 and 14). Number each section of your script to match its corresponding slide. If you plan to tape-record narration and music, you will need to play your slide show while you record the music and narration to be sure that everything fits together.

Outline of Presentation	Visual Aids	Actions	Audio
Introduction: Show title and name	Poster: How to Cook Brownies by Nicole	None	Intro Music: Beginning of "Sugar Plum Fairies"
Introduction: questions and trivia about brownies	picture looking puzzled	None	More "Sugar Plum Fairies" (softly)
Introduce materials needed	picture in kitchen with materials	None	Turn down music all the way

Introduction to Persuasive Presentations

You may have heard of the power of persuasion. The Greeks designed courses in rhetoric to teach pupils how to argue persuasively. To this day, the fine art of rhetoric is alive because politicians, lawyers, and advertisers use it every day to get us to believe and react in certain ways. Throughout history we discover great and tragic events that were inspired by a persuasive leader—the Civil Rights Act inspired by Dr. Martin Luther King, Jr. and the Holocaust instigated by Adolf Hitler are two modern examples. Court cases are now broadcast across the nation for all to view and criticize. The news depicts exciting world events and tragedies brought on by charismatic leaders. Therefore, one might learn it is not always the facts that have the most power, but it is the ways in which the facts are presented that make the argument convincing!

This section is designed to teach students the art of persuasion, using a variety of formats. However, before students are ready to conduct debates and group projects, they should try their hand at a simple persuasive essay and speech. Have students practice supporting their points with evidence by completing the exercise called *I Totally Disagree!* on page 30. Then decide on a topic or issue for the speech. You can have students *brainstorm* (page 5) issues that are important to them or assign an issue that relates to the topics you are covering in class. Once a topic has been chosen, use the *Persuasive Presentation Organizer* (page 9) to plan the essay and speech. Review the postwriting and practice activities (pages 15–19) before beginning presentations. After students have given their presentations, discuss the techniques that made some speeches more convincing than others. Have students focus on these techniques when they try another persuasive activity from this chapter.

The first persuasive activity is a debate. In *Debating the Issue* (page 31), four to eight students work together to provide persuasive arguments to support their position on an issue. For the debate activity, appoint a moderator to time each team's speaking. Allow one to three minutes for each team's turn. Make sure each student on the team is given an opportunity to support or refute an argument. You will find some debate topics listed. These may be cut out and distributed to the teams. As always, they are only a springboard to inspire you. Modify topics to suit your needs and add more. For instance, you may prefer to have topics that reinforce what is being taught in social studies, science, or literature.

In *Courtroom Drama* (page 31), students create a mock trial and try to persuade the "jury" to a verdict of guilty or not guilty through a series of questioning witnesses and making persuasive arguments. The courtroom activity will require more writing, planning, and drama than a basic debate, yet it also gets students more involved in the persuasive process. For example, you can place the Big Bad Wolf, General Custer, Socrates, or Julius Caesar on trial.

For a bit of frivolity, two activities have been included that allow students to show their dramatic flair. *Historical Commercials* (page 32) transports the speaker back in time to create a commercial for a person, place, or item from a certain period in history. The commercials can be completely original in format and slogan or spinoffs of modern advertisements. The goal of the commercial is to persuade the audience to buy a product, vote for a person, or travel to the advertised location. Students assume the identity of a character from literature or history in the activity *Character Crusaders* (page 32). In this activity they attempt to defend their actions to the audience and explain their reasoning. Students can create costumes and props to accompany their persuasive arguments. As an extension of this character portrayal, students can try their hand at improvised identify in the activity *In the Hot Seat!* (page 34).

Persuasive Presentations

I Totally Disagree!

To argue effectively, you need to prove your point with support. Support is the same thing as evidence, proof, or convincing facts to make your point. To practice supporting your point of view, fill in each of the following with three supporting ideas:

1. Why I like to laugh:
   1. _____
   2. _____
   3. _____

2. Why I like holidays:
   1. _____
   2. _____
   3. _____

3. Why I like candy:
   1. _____
   2. _____
   3. _____

4. Why I like music:
   1. _____
   2. _____
   3. _____

Now try completing the following sentences with three descriptions:

1. Yardwork is
   1. _____
   2. _____
   3. _____

2. Gum is
   1. _____
   2. _____
   3. _____

3. Homework is
   1. _____
   2. _____
   3. _____

Now pick a topic and plan to persuade your classmates. Fill in the form on page 9, and use it as an outline for a two- to three-minute persuasive speech.

Persuasive Presentations

Debating the Issue

In a debate you work in teams. One team argues their opinion while another team opposes it. Your teacher will divide your class into debate teams of four to eight students. Then you will be given a random topic from the list to debate, or a topic that relates to your other school studies. Don't be surprised if you don't agree with the position you are assigned to debate. The point is to learn to support your topic with reasonable and convincing arguments. You will be given time to prepare for the debate, so work as a group to look up facts in various references and computer encyclopedias. During the debate, take notes while the other team speaks so that you can refute their arguments with supporting evidence. Make sure every member of the team is prepared and given an opportunity to participate in the speaking. A moderator will time the speaking and let you know when your turn is over.

Debate Format:

1. Team 1 presents the topic and their position with one supporting argument.
2. Team 2 refutes the argument given by Team 1, then gives one argument for their position.
3. Team 1 refutes the argument made by Team 2, then gives a second argument for their position. (The debate continues in this manner until both sides have exhausted all of their supporting arguments.)

Debate Topics:

- Kids/parents should make the rules.
- School uniforms are a good/bad idea.
- You should drive at 16/21 years old.
- Exercise is important/a waste of time.
- A woman would/would not make a good president.
- Junk food is bad/beneficial for you.
- Watching TV is beneficial/a waste of time.
- Movies/Books are better.

Courtroom Drama

As an alternative, create a mock trial in place of a debate. Place a historical figure or character from literature on trial and try to persuade the audience or "jury" to find the character guilty or innocent of a particular crime or action. Your teacher will act as the judge to moderate the actions of the trial and call on the different people to speak. Below is the list of players and format for a mock trial:

Players:

- jury (audience)
- 2 defense lawyers for the accused
- judge (teacher)
- 3 witnesses supporting the actions of the accused
- 2 prosecution lawyers against the accused
- 3 witnesses opposing the accused

Format:

1. The judge introduces the case, the accused, and the lawyers.
2. Testimony against the accused is given by the accuser and other witnesses. After each testimony, one of the defense lawyers is allowed to cross-examine the witnesses.
3. Testimony defending the accused is given by witnesses and the accused. After each testimony, one of prosecution lawyers is allowed to cross-examine the witnesses.
4. Closing remarks are given by the lawyers on both sides.
5. Closing remarks about voting are given by the judge to the jury.
6. The jury votes, ballots are counted, and the verdict (and sentence, if guilty) are pronounced.

Persuasive Presentations

Historical Commercials

Imagine the god Hermes selling the latest Olympic sandal or George Washington persuading you to buy a pair of wooden dentures! Pretend you and some friends are an advertising company from the period in history you are studying and create a persuasive and enticing commercial. Have your group review the opening chapter on "Organizing and Preparing Presentations." Use the organizer (page 8) to help plan and sequence some appealing support to persuade the audience. Create a storyboard (page 12) for visual or audio effects and a script (pages 13 and 14) for your group, as well as costumes, props, and scenery. (See "Send In the Props," page 41). Your commercial can be about any of the following:

- an invention or tool from that time
- a political advertisement for a famous leader
- a mode of transportation
- clothing, jewelry, or hygiene products

- an advancement in medical technology
- a travel promotion to visit a certain location
- a food or beverage
- houses or other buildings

Be sure to be convincing so that the audience will want to run right out and do whatever your ad promotes. You can create your commercial as a total original or create a spinoff of a popular ad on TV. You may want to include a catchy slogan or jingle so that the audience will remember you and your product.

Character Crusaders

This activity takes persuasive speech to a dramatic level. Pretend that you are a character from history or a character from a story that was involved in a controversial event. Plan a persuasive speech supporting your actions. Use the *Persuasive Presentation Organizer* (page 9) to plan your speech with convincing supporting arguments. Add props or costumes to help appeal to the audience. Below is a list of characters and events as samples of the types of speeches that could be created:

- Moses explains why he led the Hebrews into the desert to save them from the Egyptians.
- King Nebuchadnezzar explains why he was forced to exile the Hebrews from Babylon.
- Pontius Pilate explains why he had to order the execution of Jesus to save the Roman Empire.
- Julius Caesar explains why he disobeyed orders and crossed the Rubicon.
- Brutus explains why he joined others to assassinate Julius Caesar.
- Socrates explains why he drank the hemlock instead of complying with the Greek government.
- Cleopatra explains why she killed herself instead of returning to Rome.
- Richard I explains why he joined the Crusades.

The speech could be a plea for understanding or a plea to join you in your fight. Be creative and try to take on the role of your character with your voice, stance, and gestures. Appeal to the audience for their support, using any means possible!

Introduction to Impromptu Presentations

The ability to "think on your feet" and organize your thoughts so that they can be presented clearly is a great skill to master. This skill is used every day in many professions. Yet, this ability is not easily mastered without training and practice. A student's first introduction to impromptu speaking should be simple and stressless. Often students "forget" to feel uncomfortable when distracted by a simple spontaneous improvisation. This section contains five activities to foster impromptu speaking, from the easy to the more challenging improvised scene.

First there is an activity called *What's My Word?* (page 34). This is the basic game of Charades or Pictionary using spelling or vocabulary words. This simple improvisation lesson allows students to formulate connections immediately and try to convey their message through pantomime or drawings. This activity can be played with the entire class divided into two teams or in smaller groups with different teams playing each other for the championship. Students will not only gain confidence in thinking and acting quickly but also reinforce spelling and vocabulary concepts!

Next is a dramatic improvisation in which students take on the persona of a character from literature or history. When playing *In the Hot Seat!* (page 34), one student from the class becomes a character, and the rest of the class asks the character questions related to the story or period in history. This activity allows students to demonstrate their comprehension and inference skills while practicing both dramatic and improvisational abilities. Extensions of this activity can be found in the biographical section of "Let's Be Informed" (pages 21 and 22), *Writing Dialogue* (page 38) and *News Broadcast* (page 38).

Another creative thinking activity is *Liars' Club* (page 34). During this exercise, students create definitions for artifacts and objects found in books or brought in from home. Students play in teams, attempting to baffle and confuse opponents with their stunning definitions. Students learn the importance of the speaking voice, creative wording, and presentations of objects to help sway their audience.

Once students have had a chance to practice simple improvisation, it's time to move to more challenging lessons. *Off the Cuff* (page 35) offers several topics for giving an impromptu speech. They can be cut apart and kept in a box, or you may wish your students to make up speech topics based on the concepts you are covering in class—for example, My Favorite Aspect of Ancient Egypt, Who Was the Best Leader of the Civil War? and Which Is My Favorite System in the Human Body? Have students draw a topic for on-the-spot speaking. You may decide to allow students to see their prompt five or ten minutes in advance, or you may prefer that they formulate their speech immediately in front of the class and begin within a minute or two. To help students organize their thoughts while standing, it is helpful to have displayed a poster showing the basic presentation format—introduction, main body (with at least three points), and conclusion. You can make a copy of the *Informative Presentation Organizer* (page 7) as your "thinking" poster. Students may all give their impromptu speeches in one day, or you may wish to have one or two students give impromptu speeches each day during a transition between subjects.

You will find *Drama on the Spot* (page 36) takes the concept of impromptu speaking a step further. In this activity, student teams of two or three draw a scene to act out. Each team gets a moment to discuss who will play which role and to grab a prop or two. You may wish to make up scenarios from the literature you are reading or from history lessons as well. This will help evaluate comprehension as well as improvisational skills. Extensions can be found in "Tell Me a Story" (pages 37–41).

Impromptu Presentations

What's My Word?

A quick and simple way to get comfortable in front of an audience is to play a word game. Charades is played by acting out movements and expressions to help convey a word. Pictionary is played by drawing symbols and objects on the board to help convey the word. When playing the first time, it is best to work with the entire class divided into two teams. Your teacher will choose either spelling or vocabulary words to use for the game. The words will be written on slips of paper and placed in a box. A team will begin, and a student from that team will go to the front of the class. The student will pull out a word. The teacher will check to make sure the student understands the word before beginning. The team will have three minutes to try to guess the word based on the player's actions or drawings. Points for correct guesses will be given, and teams will take turns. If a team calls out of turn or exhibits poor sportsmanship, points will be deducted. The team with the most points at the end of the game wins.

In the Hot Seat!

Another simple form of improvisation is characterization. Think of characters from a story you are reading or an event from history that you are studying. Make a list of questions that you would like to ask if you could meet these people. These questions can require direct information from the story or historical period (When were you born? What year did you sail to the New World?), or they can require inference (How did you feel when you crossed the Rubicon? What was it like walking through the agora in Athens?) Make sure you review and edit the questions for the interview with your teacher before beginning the improvisation.

A student will be selected at random to come to the front of the class and sit on a chair or stool. He or she will be assigned a character and told that he/she is going to be interviewed by the class. It is important that he/she tries to sit, speak, and respond in the manner he/she believes that character would portray. Students will use the prepared set of questions for this particular character to take turns with the interview. The person in the "hot seat" will be switched occasionally so that several students get a chance to improvise for the same character. Once the interview is complete for the first character, your teacher will move to another character from your list and repeat the procedure. At the end of the activity, discuss the techniques used that made the characters believable. Who was most convincing? Why? Who showed creativity and the ability to come up with clever and appropriate answers? What did these students do to help them improvise?

Liars' Club

Another activity to help you think on your feet is a game called Liars' Club. The class is divided into teams of four players. Each team finds unusual objects in books or at home. For each object found, the team prepares four index cards. On one index card they write the true identity of the object. On the three other cards they write "LIE." Each team should prepare cards for three to four objects. On the day of the game, one team will be chosen randomly to begin. They bring one of their objects or pictures to the teacher along with the cards. The teacher shuffles the cards and hands them to the team members. The team members get two minutes to think of a way to describe their object; one person will describe the real thing, while the other three team members will think of a convincing lie. The team members take turns describing the objects to the class. The class then votes on which description they think is the truth. If the team was able to stump the class, they earn a point. Each team gets a chance to stump the class. The team with the most points at the end is the winner.

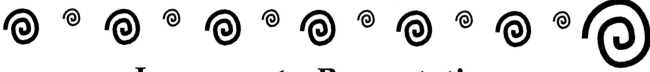

Impromptu Presentations

Off the Cuff

An impromptu speech is one that has not been prepared or rehearsed. These presentations will not be polished, perfect speeches. Have fun with them and use your imagination. (Cut the following list apart and have each student draw a topic or make up topics of your own that correspond with lessons in other subject areas.)

Why Grass Is Green	What Makes Me Really Mad
Elephants	What I Think About Aliens
What Makes People Laugh	If I Could Invent a Candy
The Best Pet to Have	Why Dogs Are Better Than Cats (or vice versa)
My History of Bicycles	Why It's Important to Read
How I Feel About Television	The Best Way to Get Exercise
My Favorite Kind of Music	My Favorite Movie
The First Time I Ever Cooked	What I Dislike About School
What I Like About School	Which Is a Better Place to Live, the Mountains or the Beach?
My Favorite Day of the Year	How to Make Lots of Money
How to Shop for a Gift	The Best Kind of Car to Drive
Marshmallows	How to Promote World Peace
My Favorite Pair of Shoes	The Best Things About Summer
A Person I Admire	What I Don't Like About Birthdays

Impromptu Presentations

Drama on the Spot

Cut these scenarios apart or design your own scenarios that correspond with your literature or history lessons. Students may draw them at random and create two- and three-character dramas. Set a timer for each dramatization so each does not go over three to five minutes.

Character #1 was driving too fast. Character #2 is a police officer.

Character #1 has just hit a baseball through character #2's window.

Character #1 wants to use the telephone to tell his or her mom that he or she will be late. Character #2 is having a long chat with a friend.

Character #1 is trying to sell an old bicycle to character #2.

Character #1 is trying to read a book, but character #2 wants to play.

Character #1 is babysitting character #2, who is very active and curious.

Character #1 has just spent hours cooking a special meal for character #2. The meal is horrible.

Character #1 has lost his or her voice and is trying to explain to character #2 why he or she can't go out on a date.

Character #1 is trying to return an article of clothing that fell apart in the washing machine. Character #2 is the store clerk.

Character #1 has just crushed the fender of the car of character #2, who happens to be the school principal.

Character #1 is visiting from another country and doesn't speak the language. He or she tries to tell characters #2 and #3 that she or he really needs to find a restroom!

Character #1 (in a fancy restaurant) is just about to ask character #2 a very important question when the waiter, character #3, drops a tray of food.

Character #1 is a schoolteacher and characters #2 and #3 are friendly students who've just come into class with poison oak rashes.

Character #1 and character #2 have just shown up at character #3's party and are dressed alike.

Character #1 just found out that he or she will be moving. Character #2 is upset. Character #3 is glad.

Characters #1 and #2 are having an argument. Character #3 wants to end it nicely.

Characters #1 and #2 go to the pet store to buy their first dog from character #3.

Characters #1, #2, and #3 have just gotten into a fender bender with each other.

Character #1 has just sprained his or her ankle on a city sidewalk. Characters #2 and #3 are passersby.

Introduction to Story Presentations

Although all civilizations have some form of dramatic storytelling today, no one knows exactly where or when the art of drama first started. Most likely drama grew from the earliest groups of storytellers around prehistoric fires. Eventually, storytelling evolved into a sophisticated form of art known as drama and could be found around the world in many different forms.

The dramatic presentations in this section are divided into three topics. The first topic, "If You Were There," contains exercises from a personal point of view. In *Writing Dialogue* (page 38), students will try their hand at expressing feelings, gestures, and dialogue appropriate for characters in a given scene. The scenes can be from literature or historical events discussed in class, or the teacher may give random scenes. Ideas for dialogue scenes can be found on page 36. This is an excellent step into drama and also an excellent way to develop writing skills. *News Broadcast* (page 38) gives your students an opportunity to tell a story through the news reporting format. Students can re-enact a short story, fairy tale, historical myth, or event from their own lives by discussing the perspectives of the different characters involved. This format not only gives a personal point of view to storytelling but also allows for interesting twists to the tales, depending on which character is doing the telling!

Don't overlook the basic art of storytelling itself! In "The Method to Our Madness" many different formats are discussed. Students will experience performing an Ancient Greek drama with masks and a chorus in *It's Greek to Me* (page 39). *Ancient Puppetry* (page 39) gives them ideas for presentations, pantomime, puppetry, and plays with visual aids and effects. *Storytelling* (page 40) is an exercise where students will learn to tell a story in an interesting and exciting way.

The final topic, "Send In the Props," presents some simple ideas for makeshift costumes, scenery, and staging. Not all dramatic presentations need elaborate props and scenery, nor do teachers always have the time to devote a month of learning to preparing for a play. Although a grand performance on stage is a wonderful and memorable lesson, it is hoped that after you view these simple options, more speaking and drama will be included in your regular daily lessons.

Before undertaking any dramatic presentation, review these tips:

1. Make sure you have planned, organized, and prepared. Use the appropriate organizer, storyboards, and scripts from the opening section (pages 4-19) for your particular dramatic format.

2. Allow ample time for planning before students actually start to "walk through" their presentation. Check over their plans and make corrections where needed.

3. Make sure students are realistic in their goals. Take into account the resources, time, and abilities of the actors when choosing a format.

4. Set up a time frame for planning, rehearsing, and presenting their drama. Some presentations may be planned, rehearsed, and presented all in the same day or period. Other presentations may take a week to a month. Set completion dates for the different components of the process. For example, "Your organizer is due _____, your rough draft script is due _____, begin practicing _____, your final presentation will be_____, etc."

5. Practice, practice, practice! Review the tips from pages 17–19 to help create successful and entertaining presentations.

Story Presentations

Writing Dialogue

A dialogue is a conversation between two or more people. Writing dialogue is different from writing scripts. Follow the directions below for an exercise in writing dialogue:

1. Read aloud from any book containing dialogue. Try to find examples with a variety of quotation techniques that show what the character was saying as well as the feelings and actions.

2. Write these three examples of quotation techniques on the board or overhead projector:

    -   **Speaker before:** Alan said triumphantly, "Now I know the truth. And it's you!" pointing to Dan.

    -   **Speaker after:** "Now I know the truth. And it's you!" said Alan triumphantly, pointing to Dan.

    -   **Speaker in between:** "Now I know the truth," said Alan triumphantly, pointing to Dan, "And it's you!"

3. Point out the different punctuation needed for each example by coloring the commas one color and the quotation marks another. Have students note the feelings and actions as well as the actual spoken words.

4. Assign students to groups of three or four. Assign dialogue scenes from page 36 or from the literature or history you are studying in class. Have students write a dialogue using a variety of quotation techniques like those above. Make sure students include the gestures, facial expressions, and feelings of the characters, as well as the spoken words.

5. Have students perform their dialogues by acting out the scene with a narrator reading the written section outside of the quotation marks while the character speaks the quotes. Discuss the scenes and the students' ability to convey the actions and feelings of the characters.

News Broadcast

A clever way to tell a story is to conduct a news broadcast of the event. In this format the story is not necessarily told from start to finish, but retold from the different perspectives of the characters. This format is best used with a familiar story, such as classic fairy tales, tall tales, historical myths, or major historical events. Small groups can conduct several broadcasts, or the entire class can produce one large broadcast, depending on the story or stories you are going to tell.

To begin, prepare a *Story Presentation Organizer* (page 11). Depending on how elaborate you plan to make the broadcast, you will need to prepare a storyboard (page 12) and script (pages 13 and 14). Discuss the format of a news program and *brainstorm* (page 5) together the different components. When planning the broadcast, include some of the following elements:

-   One or two anchor people introduce the "breaking story" and guide the story from start to finish.

-   Have on-the-spot interviews in which characters from the story tell their point of view of events.

-   Re-enact scenes as if they were "videotaped earlier that day" (or show actual video).

-   Develop catchy opening and closing phrases/theme song/music for the news program.

Story Presentations

It's Greek to Me

Naturally, any story can be told in play form. To create a play, fill out the *Story Presentation Organizer* (page 11) and follow the directions for creating a storyboard and script (pages 12–14). However, if you want a twist on the basic play format, try presenting a play like the Ancient Greeks. The Greeks had two main elements in their dramatic format: a chorus or group of narrators that helped explain the action of the story in song and dance and the actors who wore large masks to show their feelings.

Work in groups of about eight students—four for the chorus and four for the actors. Choose a story to tell or write an original story of your own. Plan and organize your play and script, using the following format:

- Introduction by the chorus who set up the premise of the story and the first scene.
- Scene 1 played by the actors.
- Discussion of Scene 1 and introduction of Scene 2 by the chorus.
- Scene 2 played by the actors.

(Continue following this pattern until all scenes are completed.)

- Closing of the play by the chorus.

The chorus can rap, sing, or speak in rhythm, using dance steps or simple choreographed movements. The actors can wear masks made from paper plates or headbands with the characters names written on them.

Ancient Puppetry

Another interesting format variation for telling a story is to use puppets. Follow the same procedure to plan, write, and edit your script and storyboard. You can tape-record the dialogue or speak live while giving the show. Below are a few ideas for making puppets. Check the Resources at the end of the book for further ideas.

- Use an old white sock and masking tape. Draw the eyes, nose, mouth, hair, etc. on masking tape with a black permanent marker. Color them with markers, cut them out, and tape them onto the sock.

- Use an empty toilet paper roll and decorate it with construction paper or fabric. You can make a finger puppet by cutting the head and body out of the roll and using your fingers for the legs.

- Use a tongue depressor and poster board to make a stick puppet. If desired, use a paper fastener and wooden skewer to make a movable arm or leg.

Story Presentations

Storytelling

The ability to tell a story that is interesting and exciting is rapidly becoming a lost art form. Try your hand at storytelling by choosing a favorite short story or fairy tale to tell to a group of students. If desired, you may want to write an original story of your own or tell about an event from your life.

To begin, plan your story by filling out a *Story Presentation Organizer* (page 11). If you are telling about an event from your own life, fill out an *Autobiographical Incident Presentation Organizer* (page 10). Follow the directions on pages 15 and 16 to write a rough draft, edit, and revise.

Practice telling your story, using the tips on pages 17-19. Remember, you are not "reading" the story word for word, but telling it. Use lots of expression, gestures, and actions to keep the attention of your audience. You may want to use different voices for the different characters as well.

Visual Aids and Effects

Sometimes when you tell a story, it is fun to use visual aids and special effects. Choose one of the methods below to enhance your storytelling presentation. You may be able to create the effect on your own, or you may use the help of an assistant or two.

Flip charts: Use large sheets of construction paper to construct a flip chart showing illustrations for key scenes in the story.

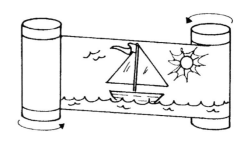

Roll stories: Use large cardboard rolls from paper towels or wrapping paper as the scrolls for your story. Attach a long sheet of butcher paper to the scrolls and draw the key scenes on the paper. Scroll the paper to display each scene as you tell the story.

Hats: Create a different hat for each character in the story. As you become the character, place the corresponding hat on your head to help show the audience who you are. Try to use a different voice for each character, as well.

Sound effects: Some stories offer situations for engaging sound effects such as walking, knocking, or snoring. As you tell the story, incorporate the different sounds. You can even have the audience help make the sounds as you tell the story. To do this, choose three or four simple sounds that are repeated throughout the story. Have the audience practice these sounds before you begin the story. Give them a key word or phrase that lets them know which sound to make. As you tell the story, emphasize the key word and make the sound with the audience. This technique is especially successful for keeping the interest of younger audiences.

Props: Bring in a few props to use to help emphasize the key actions of the story. Try to choose props that are used repeatedly throughout the story and are key elements to the plot.

Story Presentations

Overhead Projector Scenery

One quick and easy way to create a variety of scenery is to draw the scenes onto overhead projector plastic. These sheets of clear plastic can be found at most schools and at any office supply store. Draw a rough draft of your scene on regular notebook paper. The scenes should be simple yet decorative, with elements key to the story. Then trace the scene onto the clear plastic, using a black overhead marker. Try the scenery by shining it onto the wall and standing in front of it. The scenery wall should be covered in white butcher paper from floor to ceiling. (You can cover an existing bulletin board display or chalkboard temporarily, and then you can just remove the butcher paper when finished, leaving all intact!) Make adjustments to the scenery by erasing with water and redrawing the needed lines.

Once the scenery is just the way you want it, trace over the lines with permanent black marker and clean off the old marker with water. Color in the scenery, using a variety of overhead markers. To get more colors, experiment with other markers on the plastic. Some regular markers don't cover completely, and some cover so completely that you just see a shadow and not the color.

Make a sheet of scenery for each scene in your play. Another option is to create slides with a camera and slide film. Photograph scenery that would be appropriate for your story and use the slides as the backgrounds for your play. The great thing about doing scenery in this manner is that many different plays with many different scenes can be performed by using only the one wall covered in white butcher paper!

(Teacher note: When they are performing in front of the overhead or slide projector, it is important for students NOT to look directly into the light.)

Instant Costumes

Not all performances require elaborate costumes. For quick performances, have the characters' names written on large index cards and taped to the performers. You can tie yarn to the cards and hang them around the performers' necks. Headbands are another alternative. You can make a quick headband out of construction paper and write the character's name on it.

Create a Stage

Front of the Room: A stage for a performance or any presentation can be as simple as an empty area in the front or back of a classroom. Make sure the area is large enough for all characters to move around and in and out of the scene. If scenery or visual aids are needed, make sure there is a clear wall or chalkboard where those aids can be hung and seen. Some presentations also requires props, notes, etc., so make a space. A speaker's podium can be used.

Theater in the Round: Some presentations work well if the stage is in the middle of the classroom and the audience sits around the outside. This kind of play is fun because it requires no scenery and no worry that the actors are not facing the audience! Move all of the desks and tables so that there is an empty space in the middle of the room with an aisle for characters to enter and exit. Be sure to take this stage arrangement into account when writing your script and storyboard.

Table Puppet Show: Turn a table or set of desks on their sides and cover them with butcher paper. Puppeteers can sit behind the tables and conduct the show above.

Introduction to Multimedia Presentations

The activities in this section introduce students to the amazing world of multimedia. Multimedia allows students various options for presenting information and expressing themselves. Students with various capabilities and intelligences can learn to create presentations that utilize their own capacities to the maximum extent. The use of multimedia will strengthen the students' skills in researching, writing, organizing, critical thinking, problem solving, and relating and applying ideas.

The section begins with instruction in the use of *HyperStudio*® (pages 44 and 45). Other multimedia programs will be similar, but in any case, the literature and tutorials that accompany the software should be referred to for more information. The directions can be copied and used as a reference or a tutorial. Keep in mind, however, that reading about how to use multimedia can be overwhelming and possibly confusing at first. You might prefer to simply load the program and begin to experiment. This is one time when it might be better to leave the directions for later. *HyperStudio*® is user-friendly, and one can learn to create a stack without looking at a manual. After everyone has had an opportunity to explore the program, the instructions might be even more helpful.

After students have gained confidence with multimedia, they will create a book report or research project (pages 46 and 47) using *HyperStudio*®. They will find the *Hyperstack Planning Form* (page 43) to be useful, and it will allow you to determine at a glance their readiness to go on to the actual computer work. You may choose to have your students do only the book report, only the research project, or both. The book report would be good as an introduction since the subject will not require much additional research. For the research project, give your students a list of subjects. You may coordinate the research topic with your curriculum or create a list appropriate to the abilities of your students. You will also want to let them know how many cards you expect for their multimedia report.

The practice involved in producing this multimedia presentation will prove invaluable to the students in your class. Providing such activities means that you are arming students with a package of skills that will serve them well in all other subjects in school and prepare them for the requirements of the business world. Students familiar with the technology of multimedia and proficient in its use are gaining the necessary skills to become competent citizens of tomorrow and productive members of our society. The results will produce a clear and evident sense of accomplishment for the students and the teacher.

Hyperstack Planning Form

Use the form below to plan your *HyperStudio®,* or other multimedia, presentation. Be sure to include the placement of buttons, graphics, and text.

Multimedia Presentations

Getting Started

1. Once you have opened *HyperStudio®,* click the "New Stack" icon.
2. Choose "Save As" from the "File" menu, name your file, and save it.
3. Choose the "Tools" menu and click and hold the mouse button down while you drag it off to the side. Do the same with the "Colors" menu.

Creating the Cards

Background

1. Choose "Import Background" from the "File" menu.
2. Locate the HS Art folder, which is in the *HyperStudio®* folder.
3. Locate Dingbats 1, Dingbats 2, Computer 1, or Computer 2 and open one of them.
4. Click on the "Selection" tool from the toolbox. Select everything in the picture except the border. Press the Delete key.

Title

1. Choose "Add a Text Object" from the "Objects" menu.
2. When the box appears, click outside of the box.
3. Then, on the screen that appears, click "Style." You will need to choose a point size, font, and color for your title.
4. Choose "Center" where it says "Align," and then click off the Xs where it says, "Scrollable" and "Draw Scroll Bar." Click "OK."
5. Give your stack a title that includes your name, and save your work.

Clip Art

1. Choose "Clip Art" from the "File" menu.
2. Locate the HS Art folder, choose one of the art cards in the folder, and open it.
3. When you have the picture you want, select the lasso tool and circle the part of the picture you want, and then click "OK." Note: If the card you choose does not have a picture you want, click on "Get another picture."
4. When you find a picture you want, repeat step 3.
5. When the picture you choose appears on the screen, use the mouse and drag it to where you want it on the screen.

The Button

1. Choose "Add a Button" from the "Objects" menu.
2. You now have several choices to make. You can make the text and background of your button match the color of your stack. You also need to put some text on your button so anyone looking at your stack will know how the button should be used. For instance, "Next Card" can be typed in the name box.
3. When selecting your button shape, choose only from the top four button shapes on the top left corner of the dialogue box.
4. After you have chosen a button shape, click on "Icons" and choose an icon to go inside your button. Be sure all three boxes have Xs on the bottom left of the dialogue box. Click "OK."

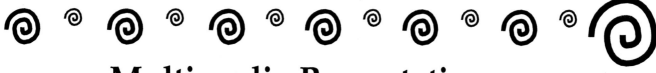

Multimedia Presentations *(cont.)*

The Button *(cont.)*

5. When the button appears on your card, use the mouse to drag it to where you want it and then click outside of the button to place it.

6. After you place your button, the "Actions" dialogue box will appear. Then on the left side of the box, under "Places to Go," choose "Another Card." When the next box comes up, choose the left or right arrow and click "OK."

7. Finally, select a transition. Click on "Try It" before clicking "OK." If you like it, click "OK."

8. To begin the next card in your stack, choose "New Card" from the "Edit" menu.

To Animate

1. Use a pencil tool or a paintbrush tool from the toolbox to draw a picture to animate. Use the paint bucket tool to fill your picture with the color you choose.

2. To animate, choose "Add a Button" from the "Objects" menu. Choose the button color and put text on the button (for example, "Animate 1"). Choose a button shape.

3. Drag the button into place with the mouse, click outside of the button, and the "Actions" dialogue box will appear. Under "Things to Do," choose "New Button Actions."

4. When the "New Button Actions" dialogue box appears, click on "Animator," and then click on "Use This NBA."

5. When the next screen appears, click on the lasso, and then click on "From the Screen." Lasso the entire picture or the part of the picture you want to move. Move the picture where you want it and then click the mouse.

6. When the dialogue box comes back, click on "Hide Background" on the first frame and click "OK" twice. Try out your new button!

To Add Text

1. Choose "Add a Text Object" from the "Objects" menu. When the text box appears, click outside of it, and that will cause the "Text Appearances" dialogue box to appear.

2. Choose "Style." When the next box appears, select a font, point size, and a color. Click "OK."

3. Type your text. If you want the scroll box bar to appear, fill the text box. Then you can add a scrolling button by choosing "Add a Button" from the "Objects" menu.

4. Choose your colors and text for your buttons ("Scroll").

5. Next you will need to choose your "New Button Actions" ("Roll Credits") and choose a scrolling speed.

The Last Button

1. Follow the directions above to choose colors, icon, text, and background for your button. Your last button will be named "Beginning," "Home," or possibly "Table of Contents."

2. Experiment with *HyperStudio*®. You can go back into your cards and add more clip art. You can add sound to a button. You can paint the background a different color. You can get graphics from The Writing Center of the Scrapbook. Try different things and explore. It's easy to start over if you don't like the results.

Multimedia Book Report or Research Project

Now that you have practiced using multimedia, here is your opportunity to create a report and/or project. You will be able to make your report and/or project "come alive" with the advantages of multimedia.

Create your first card as a title page and home page. On this card you will want to include the title of the book or your project, the author's name, and your name. Also include any graphics you want. Add buttons to lead viewers to the other cards in your stack. For instance, if your book report is on *Little House on the Prairie,* you might want a button labeled "About the Author" to lead to a card about Laura Ingalls Wilder. You might also want to include any of the following buttons: "Other Books by Laura Ingalls Wilder," "Prairie Life," "Excerpts from the Book," and/or "What I Like About the Book." If someone were to click on the "About the Author" button, he or she might find something like the following: a photograph of Laura Ingalls Wilder, a scrollable biography, background art of her environment, and, perhaps, a video clip of the author speaking. There might be a segment from the television series depicting Laura or possibly an audio clip of music from the television program. Also, on this card, you will need a "Home" button so that persons exploring your hyperstack can go back to the first card (the title/home card). Then they can click on another button to explore further.

When you create a multimedia research project, choosing a topic may be the most difficult part even when your teacher gives you guidelines. Pick a topic that will really shine with multimedia. For instance, if you were to pick the topic of Dr. Martin Luther King, Jr., you would find quotations, photographs, video clips, and biographical information. You would also find a great deal of related material on the civil rights movement, black history, nonviolent civil disobedience, prejudice, and slavery.

Begin by planning what information you will include. An outline would be a good idea, but you may use whatever organizational form you prefer. Using notecards to collect information works especially well with multimedia because you will be creating cards on the computer. Arrange the cards according to topic, and then when you have collected and organized your information, use the note cards to plan each hyperstack card. You may prefer to use the *Hyperstack Planning Form* (page 43).

Multimedia Book Report or
Research Project *(cont.)*

Once you have a plan in place, it will be time to create the first card in your stack. Your teacher will tell you how many cards are expected, so plan accordingly.

As with other *HyperStudio®* presentations, consider your first card to be the cover of your report. For this report, you can put the title on this card, your name, art, and just one button. Your button may be titled "Click here" or "Contents."

Your second card will be your table of contents. You will need to decide whether you want viewers of your report to go through each card in sequence or if you want them to be able to choose where they want to go and be able to return to the contents. Usually, you will want them to be able to do the latter. It is more fun and more interesting to be able to explore. Assign a button for each section of your report and don't forget a button to go back to the cover so viewers can exit when finished. You can title it "Exit." If there is room, you can add graphics and a video clip.

The rest of your cards will be dedicated to your subtopics. For instance, your might have a card that is listed in the table of contents as "Quotations." When that button is clicked on, the "Quotations" card will appear. If your report is on Dr. Martin Luther King, Jr., you could have scrollable text of the "I Have a Dream" speech on this card. You might have a quotation across the card as background, along with a photograph or drawing of Dr. King. You would definitely want a video clip of Dr. Martin Luther King, Jr. delivering a speech. There are many options, and it will be up to you. Be sure to include on each card a button that will take the viewer back to the table of contents. The button can be labeled "Table of Contents," "Contents," "Back," "Exit," or whatever will indicate that clicking that button will lead back to the beginning.

For your final card, you will create a bibliography. This is a time when you will take full advantage of the scroll bar. You will be able to put an entire bibliography in a window which the viewer can scroll. That will leave room on your final page for some more art or a final video, if you like. You might also want to use this page to give credit for any photographs or videos you used. If you have a list, you might want to put the credits in another window with a scroll bar. Be sure to include on your final page a button that will lead back to the table of contents or title page. You do not want your viewers to get stuck on your last page. You want them to be able to go back and take another look at an interesting page.

When you have completed a multimedia report, congratulate yourself. You have really accomplished something! Now you can say with confidence, "I can give a presentation!"

Resources

Books

Borman, Jaime Lynee. *Computer Dictionary for Kids. . . and Their Parents.* Barron's Educational Series, Inc., 1995.

Bryant, Mary Helen. *Integrating Technology into the Curriculum.* Teacher Created Resources, Inc., 1996.

Creegan, George. *Sir George's Book of Hand Puppetry.* Follett Publishing Company, 1966.

Dana, Ann, Marianne Handler, and Jane Peters Moore. *Hypermedia as a Student Tool: A Guide for Teachers.* Teacher Ideas Press, 1995.

Dunbar, Robert E. *How to Debate.* Franklin Watts, 1994.

Fontaine, Robert. *Humorous Skits for Young People.* Plays, Inc., 1970.

Gilford, Henry. *How to Give a Speech.* Franklin Watts, 1980.

Hayes, Deborah Shepherd. *Managing Technology in the Classroom.* Teacher Created Resources, Inc., 1995.

Hayes, Deborah Shepherd. *Multimedia Projects.* Teacher Created Resources, Inc., 1997.

LeBaron, John and Philip Miller. *Portable Video: A Production Guide for Young People.* Prentice-Hall, Inc., 1982.

Mandell, Muriel. *Games to Learn By.* Sterling Publishing Co., Inc., (Oak Tree Press Co., Ltd; London & Sydney), 1973.

McBride, Karen Hein and Elizabeth Deboer Luntz. *Help! I Have HyperStudio...Now What Do I Do?* McBride Media, 1996.

Miller, Helen Louise. *First Plays for Children.* Plays, Inc., 1985.

Pereira, Linda. *Computers Don't Byte.* Teacher Created Resources, Inc., 1996.

Philpott, A.R., ed. *Eight Plays for Hand Puppets.* Plays, Inc., 1972.

Seto, Judith Roberts. *The Young Actor's Workbook.* Grove Press, Inc., 1984.

Supraner, Robyn and Lauren Supraner. *Plenty of Puppets to Make.* Troll Associates, 1981.

Wallace, Mary. *I Can Make Puppets.* Owl Books, 1994.

Wodaski, Ron. *Absolute Beginner's Guide to Multimedia.* Sams Publishing, 1994.

Yerian, Cameron and Margaret, ed. *Fun Time Plays and Special Effects.* Children's Press, 1975.

Software

HyperStudio 3.0. Roger Wagner Publishing, Inc., 1050 Pioneer Way, Suite P., El Cajon, CA 92020. 1-800-421-6526.

Kid Pix 2. Broderbund Software Direct, P.O. Box 6125, Novato, CA 94948-6125. 1-800-474-8840.

Multimedia Workshop. Davidson and Associates, 19840 Pioneer Ave., Torrance, CA 90503. 1-800-545-7677.